中文百宝箱
CHINESE TREASURE CHEST

农历新年
Chinese New Year

(Simplified Chinese)

T0343869

学生用书
Student
Workbook

林宛芊　　马慕贞　　傅爱玫
Marisa Fang　**Helen Jung**　**Rosemary Firestein**

CENGAGE

Australia • Brazil • Mexico • Singapore • United Kingdom • United States

**Chinese Treasure Chest:
Chinese New Year
Student Workbook
(Simplified Chinese)**

**Marisa Fang
Helen Jung
Rosemary Firestein**

Regional Director, Marketing:
Melissa Chan

Senior Marketing Manager:
Lee Hong Tan

Senior Editorial Manager:
Lian Siew Han

Assistant Editorial Manager:
Tanmayee Bhatwadekar

Development Editors:
Titus Teo
Kenneth Chow
Wei Yi Ng
Elaine Chew
Cecile Zhang
Iris Poh

Associate Development Editor:
Dawn Chaim

Senior Regional Manager,
Production and Rights:
Pauline Lim

Production Executive:
Rachael Tan

Senior Graphic Designer:
Toon Check Foo

Compositor:
Sok Ling Ong

Illustrator:
Han Boon Ng

For product information and technology assistance, contact us at
Cengage Learning Asia Customer Support, 65-6410-1200

For permission to use material from this text or product,
submit all requests online at **www.cengageasia.com/permissions**
Further permissions questions can be emailed to
asia.permissionrequest@cengage.com

Print Edition
ISBN: 978-981-4846-97-4

Digital Edition
ISBN: 978-981-4866-73-6

Cengage Learning Asia Pte Ltd
151 Lorong Chuan #02-08
New Tech Park (Lobby H)
Singapore 556741

Cengage Learning is a leading provider of customized learning solutions with office locations around the globe, including Singapore, the United Kingdom, Australia, Mexico, Brazil, and Japan. Locate your local office at **www.cengage.com**

Cengage Learning products are represented in Canada by Nelson Education, Ltd.

To learn more about Cengage Learning Solutions, visit **www.cengageasia.com**

Every effort has been made to trace all sources and copyright holders of copyrighted material in this book before publication, but if any have been inadvertently overlooked, the publisher will ensure that full credit is given at the earliest opportunity.

Printed in Singapore
Print Number: 02   Print Year: 2020

Preface

Our **Chinese New Year Student Workbook** is a fantastic collection of materials for students to explore the rich traditions of China's most popular holiday, and, at the same time, enhance their Chinese proficiency level. This special workbook edition will help students learn about all aspects of the entire Chinese New Year Festival. This workbook can be used by individual students or groups of students in schools or cultural programs.

The activities for each topic are clearly defined by their level of difficulty (Beginner ☆, Beginner-Intermediate ☾, Intermediate ☆☾, Intermediate-Advanced ☾○, Advanced ○, All ☺). Activities marked with the 🔊 icon include audio recordings that can help students improve their listening and speaking skills. These recordings are available at **http://emarketing.cengageasia.com/cnywb**. There are also activities that focus on strengthening reading and writing skills.

Highlights of the workbook include stories about the 12 Zodiac Animals. Activities such as puzzles, songs, riddles, and mini-books all support students to gain a deeper understanding of these significant cultural legends.

Creating hands-on arts and crafts projects such as lanterns, lion and dragon puppets, paper firecrackers will provide entertainment for students as well as a clear vision about the customs and traditions that are important to people in Chinese communities. Additionally, names of Zodiac animals, Chinese New Year foods, and traditional Chinese New Year greetings are presented in various activities so that students can become proficient in speaking about these topics.

Lastly, a section of the student book focuses on learning Chinese characters related to Chinese New Year. The characters are attractively displayed with illustrations and stroke order directions for students to practice.

We are sure that students will have fun while learning with our **Chinese New Year Student Workbook**! Best wishes for a Happy Chinese New Year!

Marisa Fang (林宛芊)

Helen Jung (马慕贞)

Rosemary Firestein (傅爱玫)

New York, USA

Table of Contents
目录

☆ Beginner   ☾ Intermediate   ☆☾ Beginner-Intermediate   ☾○ Intermediate-Advanced   ○ Advanced   ☺ All

☆ Beginner　☾ Intermediate　☆☾ Beginner-Intermediate　☾○ Intermediate-Advanced　○ Advanced　☺ All

shí 十 èr 二 shēng 生 xiào 肖

名字：＿＿＿＿

＿＿＿年　＿＿＿月　＿＿＿日

xīng qī rì 星期日	xīng qī yī 星期一	xīng qī èr 星期二	xīng qī sān 星期三	xīng qī sì 星期四	xīng qī wǔ 星期五	xīng qī liù 星期六

What's Happening in This Month?
这个月知多少?

1. <ruby>今<rt>jīn</rt></ruby> <ruby>天<rt>tiān</rt></ruby> <ruby>是<rt>shì</rt></ruby>_____ <ruby>月<rt>yuè</rt></ruby> _____ <ruby>日<rt>rì</rt></ruby> 。

2. <ruby>明<rt>míng</rt></ruby> <ruby>天<rt>tiān</rt></ruby> <ruby>是<rt>shì</rt></ruby>_____ <ruby>月<rt>yuè</rt></ruby> _____ <ruby>日<rt>rì</rt></ruby> 。

3. <ruby>昨<rt>zuó</rt></ruby> <ruby>天<rt>tiān</rt></ruby> <ruby>是<rt>shì</rt></ruby>_____ <ruby>月<rt>yuè</rt></ruby> _____ <ruby>日<rt>rì</rt></ruby> 。

4. <ruby>今<rt>jīn</rt></ruby> <ruby>天<rt>tiān</rt></ruby> <ruby>是<rt>shì</rt></ruby> <ruby>星<rt>xīng</rt></ruby> <ruby>期<rt>qī</rt></ruby>_____ 。

5. <ruby>这<rt>zhè</rt></ruby> <ruby>个<rt>ge</rt></ruby> <ruby>月<rt>yuè</rt></ruby> <ruby>有<rt>yǒu</rt></ruby>_____ <ruby>天<rt>tiān</rt></ruby>

6. <ruby>这<rt>zhè</rt></ruby> <ruby>个<rt>ge</rt></ruby> <ruby>月<rt>yuè</rt></ruby> <ruby>中<rt>zhōng</rt></ruby> <ruby>特<rt>tè</rt></ruby> <ruby>别<rt>bié</rt></ruby> <ruby>的<rt>de</rt></ruby> <ruby>日<rt>rì</rt></ruby> <ruby>子<rt>zi</rt></ruby> <ruby>是<rt>shì</rt></ruby>_____ 。

7. <ruby>新<rt>xīn</rt></ruby> <ruby>年<rt>nián</rt></ruby> <ruby>是<rt>shì</rt></ruby>_____ <ruby>月<rt>yuè</rt></ruby> _____ <ruby>日<rt>rì</rt></ruby> 。

8. <ruby>这<rt>zhè</rt></ruby> <ruby>个<rt>ge</rt></ruby> <ruby>月<rt>yuè</rt></ruby> <ruby>的<rt>de</rt></ruby> <ruby>第<rt>dì</rt></ruby> <ruby>一<rt>yī</rt></ruby> <ruby>个<rt>gè</rt></ruby> <ruby>星<rt>xīng</rt></ruby> <ruby>期<rt>qī</rt></ruby> <ruby>五<rt>wǔ</rt></ruby> <ruby>是<rt>shì</rt></ruby>____ <ruby>月<rt>yuè</rt></ruby> ____ <ruby>日<rt>rì</rt></ruby> 。

9. <ruby>这<rt>zhè</rt></ruby> <ruby>个<rt>ge</rt></ruby> <ruby>月<rt>yuè</rt></ruby> <ruby>的<rt>de</rt></ruby> <ruby>最<rt>zuì</rt></ruby> <ruby>后<rt>hòu</rt></ruby> <ruby>一<rt>yí</rt></ruby> <ruby>个<rt>gè</rt></ruby> <ruby>星<rt>xīng</rt></ruby> <ruby>期<rt>qī</rt></ruby> <ruby>一<rt>yī</rt></ruby> <ruby>是<rt>shì</rt></ruby>____ <ruby>月<rt>yuè</rt></ruby> ____ <ruby>日<rt>rì</rt></ruby> 。

10. _____ <ruby>的<rt>de</rt></ruby> <ruby>生<rt>shēng</rt></ruby> <ruby>日<rt>rì</rt></ruby> <ruby>是<rt>shì</rt></ruby>____ <ruby>月<rt>yuè</rt></ruby> ____ <ruby>日<rt>rì</rt></ruby> 。
   (a person's name)

shǔ lǎo shǔ 鼠/老鼠	niú 牛	hǔ lǎo hǔ 虎/老虎	tù tù zi 兔/兔子
lóng 龙	shé 蛇	mǎ 马	yáng 羊
hóu hóu zi 猴/猴子	jī 鸡	gǒu 狗	zhū 猪

Find and Color: Who Are the Winners?
找一找，涂一涂：谁赢了？

The emperor announced, "The first 12 animals to reach the finish line will have a year named after them!" Color the 12 animals who won the race. Write the numbers 1-12 next to those animals to indicate their place order.

Song: Zodiac Animals
儿歌：十二生肖

(Melody: Twinkle, Twinkle, Little Star)

shǔ niú hǔ tù　　lóng shé mǎ yáng
鼠 牛 虎 兔，　龙 蛇 马 羊，
(Twinkle, twinkle, little star,)

hóu jī gǒu zhū　　shí èr shēng xiào
猴 鸡 狗 猪，　十 二 生 肖。
(How I wonder what you are.)

lǎo shǔ dì yī　　zhū zài zuì hòu
老 鼠 第 一，　猪 在 最 后。
(Up above the world so high,)

nǐ shǔ shén me　　qǐng gào su wǒ
你 属 什 么，　请 告 诉 我。
(Like a diamond in the sky.)

shǔ niú hǔ tù　　lóng shé mǎ yáng
鼠 牛 虎 兔，　龙 蛇 马 羊，
(Twinkle, twinkle little star,)

hóu jī gǒu zhū　　shí èr shēng xiào
猴 鸡 狗 猪，　十 二 生 肖。
(How I wonder what you are!)

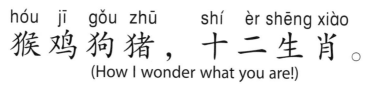

Rhyme: 12 Zodiac Animals
数来宝：十二属相

shí èr shǔ xiàng
十二属相

yí gè rén　　yǒu yí gè
一个人，有一个，

měi jiā dōu yǒu hǎo jǐ gè
每家都有好几个。

shí èr shǔ xiàng shí èr gè
十二属相十二个，

xiǎo péng yǒu zì jǐ shǔ shén me
小朋友自己属什么？

shǔ dì yī　　niú dì èr
鼠第一、牛第二、

sān hǔ　　sì tù zài yí kuài
三虎、四兔在一块；

lóng dì wǔ　　shé dì liù
龙第五、蛇第六、

qī mǎ　　bā yáng　　hóu dì jiǔ
七马、八羊、猴第九，

shí shì gōng jī　　shí yī shì gǒu
十是公鸡、十一是狗，

shí èr lǎo zhū gēn zhe zǒu
十二老猪跟着走！

yī èr yī　　zǒu yì pái
一二一，走一排，

shí èr shǔ xiàng hái jiē zhe lái
十二属相还接着来。

xiǎng zhī dào nǐ shǔ shén me
想知道你属什么？

huí jiā qù wèn lǎo nǎi nai
回家去问老奶奶！

名字：＿＿＿＿＿＿＿＿＿＿　　＿＿＿月＿＿＿日

shí èr shēng xiào
十二生肖

shǔ niú hǔ tù lóng shé mǎ yáng hóu jī gǒu zhū
鼠牛虎兔龙蛇马羊猴鸡狗猪

shǔ niú hǔ tù lóng shé mǎ yáng hóu jī gǒu zhū
鼠牛虎兔龙蛇马羊猴鸡狗猪

xiǎo xiǎo lǎo shǔ ài zuān dòng
小小老鼠爱钻洞

niú bó bo qín zuò gōng
牛伯伯勤做工

lǎo hǔ xiān sheng zhēn wēi fēng
老虎先生真威风

xiǎo bái tù ài chī luó bo
小白兔爱吃萝卜

shǔ niú hǔ tù lóng shé mǎ yáng hóu jī gǒu zhū
鼠牛虎兔龙蛇马羊猴鸡狗猪

shǔ niú hǔ tù lóng shé mǎ yáng hóu jī gǒu zhū
鼠牛虎兔龙蛇马羊猴鸡狗猪

lóng yé ye tiān shang fēi fēi fēi
龙爷爷天上飞飞飞

xiǎo shé jiě jie niǔ niǔ niǔ
小蛇姐姐扭扭扭

xiǎo mǎ gē ge dào chù pǎo
小马哥哥到处跑

xiǎo yáng mèi mei ài chī cǎo
小羊妹妹爱吃草

shǔ niú hǔ tù lóng shé mǎ yáng hóu jī gǒu zhū
鼠牛虎兔龙蛇马羊猴鸡狗猪

shǔ niú hǔ tù lóng shé mǎ yáng hóu jī gǒu zhū
鼠牛虎兔龙蛇马羊猴鸡狗猪

hóu zi shū shu ài tiào wǔ
猴子叔叔爱跳舞

jī pó po gū gū gū
鸡婆婆咕咕咕

xiǎo gǒu dì di wāng wāng wāng
小狗弟弟汪汪汪

xiǎo zhū bǎo bao gòu gòu gòu
小猪宝宝购购购

shǔ niú hǔ tù lóng shé mǎ yáng hóu jī gǒu zhū
鼠牛虎兔龙蛇马羊猴鸡狗猪

shǔ niú hǔ tù lóng shé mǎ yáng hóu jī gǒu zhū
鼠牛虎兔龙蛇马羊猴鸡狗猪

Matching Activity: Zodiac Animal Matching
配对游戏：生肖配一配

Cut out the pinyin words and Chinese characters below. Paste each next to its animal picture.

	Pinyin	Chinese Character

lǎo shǔ	lóng	mǎ	gǒu	yáng	niú
龙	狗	羊	牛	老鼠	马

Compare: Are They the Same or Different?
说一说，比一比：它们哪里相同？哪里不同？

Say the names of the following animals. Then compare each pair of animals listed below and write about their similarities and differences. The first one has been done for you. For the last question, fill in any two animals and compare them.

1.牛和羊：牛和羊都有四只脚、都吃草、颜色不同。

2.龙和蛇：＿＿＿＿＿＿＿＿＿＿＿＿＿＿＿＿＿＿＿＿＿

3.鸡和兔：＿＿＿＿＿＿＿＿＿＿＿＿＿＿＿＿＿＿＿＿＿

4.老虎和猴子：＿＿＿＿＿＿＿＿＿＿＿＿＿＿＿＿＿＿＿

5.老鼠和牛：＿＿＿＿＿＿＿＿＿＿＿＿＿＿＿＿＿＿＿＿

6.＿＿＿＿＿＿＿：＿＿＿＿＿＿＿＿＿＿＿＿＿＿＿＿＿

Bonus: Can you use two zodiac animals to make up a Chinese idiom?
Hint: Try an online search of "Chinese idioms".

jī   fēi   gǒu   tiào
(For example: 鸡飞狗跳)

1.＿＿＿＿＿＿＿＿＿＿＿＿＿＿　2.＿＿＿＿＿＿＿＿＿＿＿＿＿＿

Vocabulary Review: Who Am I?
词汇练习：我是谁？

Fill in the blanks.

wǒ shuō　　wō wō wō 1. 我说："喔喔喔……"	wǒ shì 我是＿＿＿＿＿＿＿＿＿＿＿＿。
māo ài zhuī wǒ 2. 猫爱追我。	我是＿＿＿＿＿＿＿＿＿＿＿＿。
wǒ huì fēi 3. 我会飞。	我是＿＿＿＿＿＿＿＿＿＿＿＿。
wǒ huì pá shān 4. 我会爬山。	我是＿＿＿＿＿＿＿＿＿＿＿＿。
wǒ de　bèi ràng rén qí 5. 我的背让人骑。	我是＿＿＿＿＿＿＿＿＿＿＿＿。
wǒ　ài shuì jiào 6. 我爱睡觉。	我是＿＿＿＿＿＿＿＿＿＿＿＿。
wǒ jiào　　sī sī sī 7. 我叫："嘶嘶嘶……"	我是＿＿＿＿＿＿＿＿＿＿＿＿。
wǒ ài chī hú luó bo 8. 我爱吃胡萝卜。	我是＿＿＿＿＿＿＿＿＿＿＿＿。
wǒ shuō　　miē miē miē 9. 我说："咩咩咩……"	我是＿＿＿＿＿＿＿＿＿＿＿＿。
wǒ jiào　　wāng wāng wāng 10. 我叫："汪汪汪……"	我是＿＿＿＿＿＿＿＿＿＿＿＿。
wǒ shuō　　mōu mōu mōu 11. 我说："哞哞哞……"	我是＿＿＿＿＿＿＿＿＿＿＿＿。
wǒ　ài chī xiāng jiāo 12. 我爱吃香蕉。	我是＿＿＿＿＿＿＿＿＿＿＿＿。

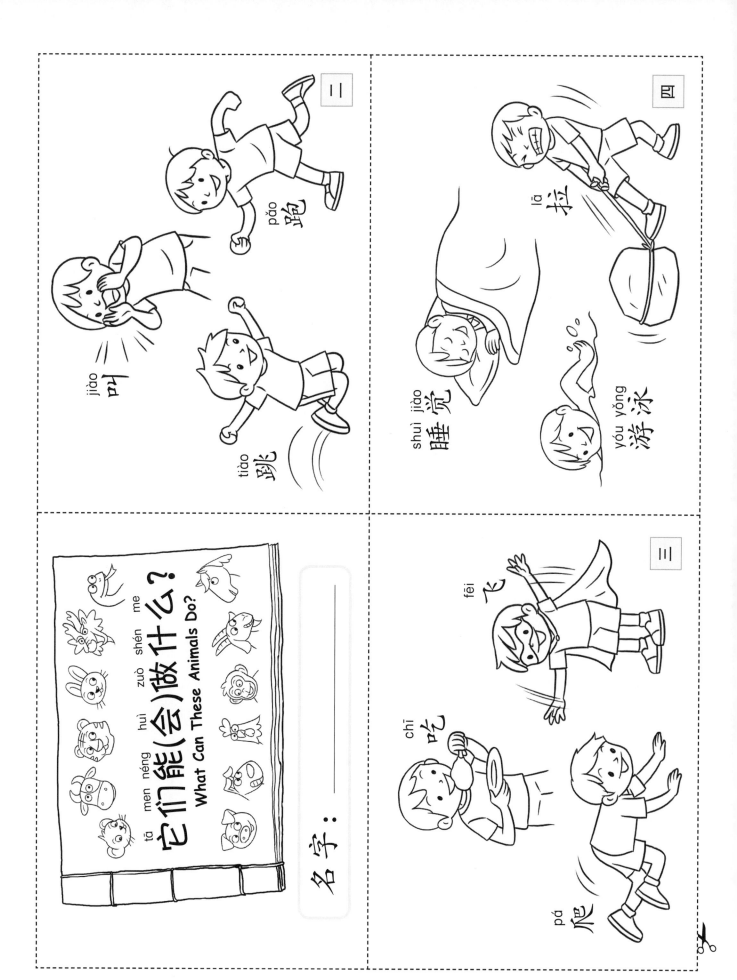

六

niú
牛

niú huì
牛会 — 车。
chē

The ox can pull a cart.

八

tù
兔

tù zi huì
兔子会 — 。

The rabbit can jump.

五

shǔ
鼠

lǎo shǔ ài
老鼠爱 — 乳酪。
rǔ lào

The rat loves to eat cheese.

七

hǔ
虎

lǎo hǔ huì
老虎会 — 山。
shān

The tiger can climb mountains.

Note: Besides "乳酪", "cheese" is also known as "起士".
qǐ shì

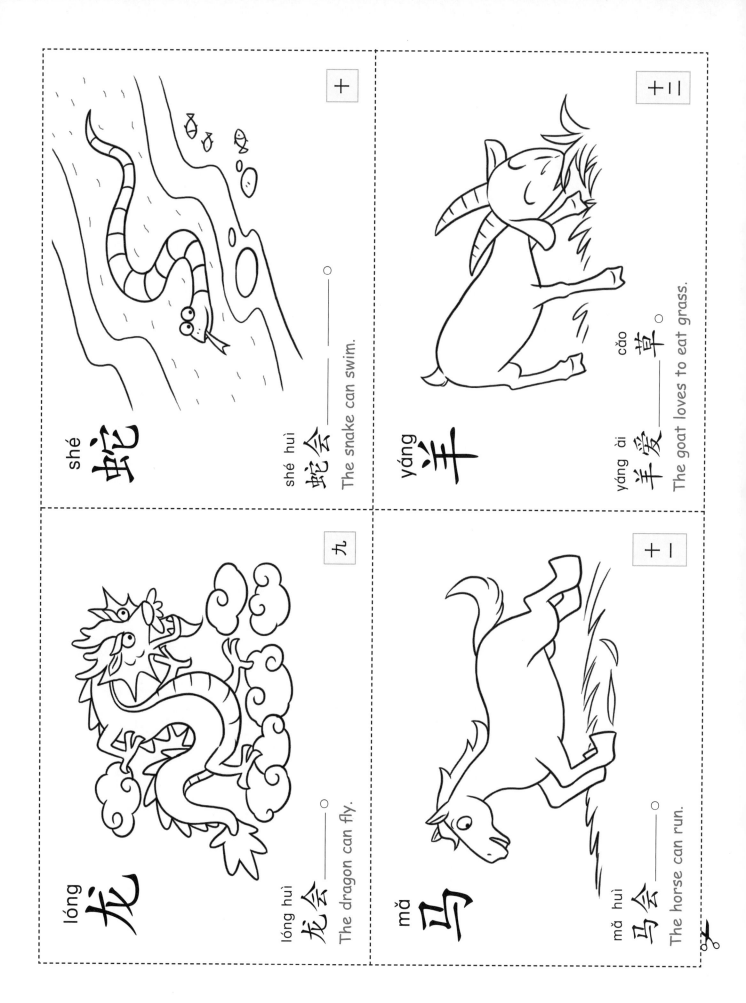

shé
蛇

shé huì
蛇会 ——○
The snake can swim.

yáng
羊

yáng ài   cǎo
羊爱 —— 草。○
The goat loves to eat grass.

lóng
龙

lóng huì
龙会 ——○
The dragon can fly.

mǎ
马

mǎ huì
马会 ——○
The horse can run.

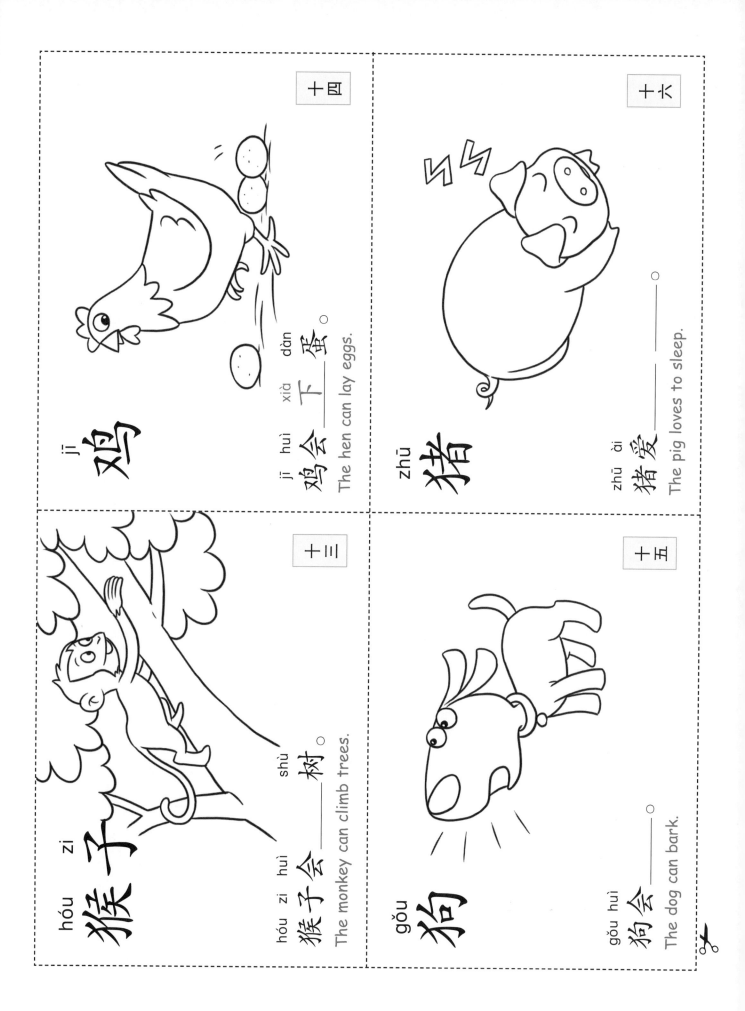

十四

jī
鸡

jī huì xià dàn
鸡会下蛋。
The hen can lay eggs.

十六

zhū
猪

zhū ài
猪爱
The pig loves to sleep.

十三

hóu zi
猴子

hóu zi huì shù
猴子会 树。
The monkey can climb trees.

十五

gǒu
狗

gǒu huì
狗会
The dog can bark.

名字：_____　_____月_____日

shǔ
鼠

1972, 1984, 1996, 2008, 2020
You are quick-witted, smart, and practical.

niú
牛

1973, 1985, 1997, 2009, 2021
You are hard working, fair-minded, and confident.

hǔ
虎

1974, 1986, 1998, 2010, 2022
You are brave, competitive, and passionate.

tù
兔

1975, 1987, 1999, 2011, 2023
You are compassionate, gentle, and quiet.

lóng
龙

1976, 1988, 2000, 2012, 2024
You are energetic, fearless, and warm-hearted.

shé
蛇

1977, 1989, 2001, 2013, 2025
You are wise, private, and intuitive.

mǎ
马

1978, 1990, 2002, 2014, 2026
You are cheerful, well-spoken, and independent.

yáng
羊

1979, 1991, 2003, 2015, 2027
You are considerate, polite, and calm.

hóu
猴

1980, 1992, 2004, 2016, 2028
You are clever, curious, and fun-loving.

jī
鸡

1981, 1993, 2005, 2017, 2029
You are responsible, honest, and organized.

gǒu
狗

1982, 1994, 2006, 2018, 2030
You are loyal, faithful, and friendly.

zhū
猪

1983, 1995, 2007, 2019, 2031
You are optimistic, social, and generous.

Math Skills: Fill in the Missing Zodiac Animal Years
算一算：填写生肖年份

Add or subtract 12 to the years provided to find the missing years for each zodiac animal.

鼠年是：＿＿＿＿，1984，＿＿＿＿，2008，＿＿＿＿。

龙年是：＿＿＿＿，1988，2000，＿＿＿＿，＿＿＿＿。

马年是：1978，＿＿＿＿，＿＿＿＿，＿＿＿＿，＿＿＿＿。

猴年是：＿＿＿＿，＿＿＿＿，2004，＿＿＿＿，＿＿＿＿。

牛年是：＿＿＿＿，＿＿＿＿，＿＿＿＿，2009，＿＿＿＿。

蛇年是：＿＿＿＿，1989，＿＿＿＿，＿＿＿＿，＿＿＿＿。

猪年是：＿＿＿＿，＿＿＿＿，＿＿＿＿，＿＿＿＿，2031。

问：马克是 2010 年生的。他属什么？
答：他属＿＿＿＿＿＿＿。

问：马克的姐姐比他大三岁。他姐姐是哪一年生的？属什么？
答：马克的姐姐是＿＿＿＿＿＿年生的。她属＿＿＿＿＿＿。

Writing Activity: What Zodiac Animal Sign Do They Have?
写一写：他们属什么生肖？

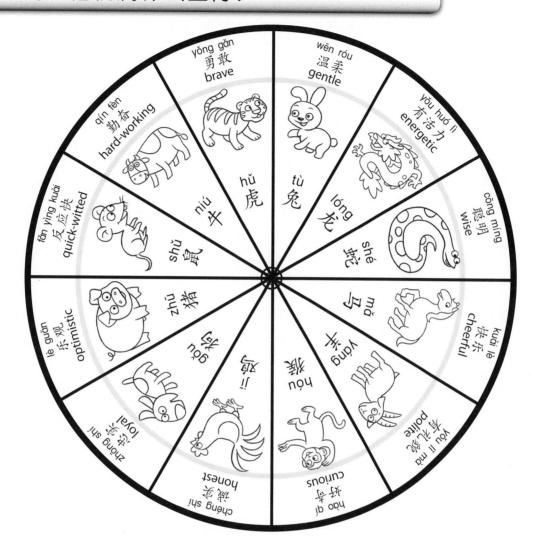

What zodiac animal sign do your family and friends have? Fill in the blanks.

1. 我属＿＿＿＿＿。我很 ＿＿＿＿＿。

   I was born.... I am very ＿＿＿＿＿.

2. 我的＿＿＿＿＿属＿＿＿＿＿。他／她很＿＿＿＿＿。

   My... was born.... He/She is very ＿＿＿＿＿.

3. 我的＿＿＿＿＿属＿＿＿＿＿。他／她很＿＿＿＿＿。

   My... was born.... He/She is very ＿＿＿＿＿.

Word Search: Zodiac Animals ❶
找一找：生肖 ❶

Write the animal names in English:

1. 猪 zhū: ＿＿＿＿＿＿＿＿＿＿

2. 老虎 lǎo hǔ: ＿＿＿＿＿＿＿＿＿＿

3. 鸡 jī: ＿＿＿＿＿＿＿＿＿＿

4. 老鼠 lǎo shǔ: ＿＿＿＿＿＿＿＿＿＿

5. 马 mǎ: ＿＿＿＿＿＿＿＿＿＿

6. 兔子 tù zi: ＿＿＿＿＿＿＿＿＿＿

7. 牛 niú: ＿＿＿＿＿＿＿＿＿＿

8. 蛇 shé: ＿＿＿＿＿＿＿＿＿＿

9. 龙 lóng: ＿＿＿＿＿＿＿＿＿＿

10. 猴子 hóu zi: ＿＿＿＿＿＿＿＿＿＿

11. 羊 yáng: ＿＿＿＿＿＿＿＿＿＿

12. 狗 gǒu: ＿＿＿＿＿＿＿＿＿＿

Find the above pinyin words in the word search puzzle below.

```
c j l m z k l i g t c i a
g n i e o a a a x b k w z
c l u t d i d m o l y h c
n i l e i a m e d h u o e
n t e k a g e m l n u u g
h a x h c y c d y a n z b
g p k e p g t y l g d i h
x y a n g y u g o u j t m
p w d s y h j m n s a c a
k b x i s i b e g u b u e
c s d o a y e k m l y d h
l v a e x h y c m t i h b
i l y d h c o g o z h a g
h s g m u s t x u j o l c
k d y h u m k t o h d j e
```

Word Search: Zodiac Animals ❷
找一找：生肖 ⬤

How many times can you find these animal names in the word search?
Fill in the blanks.

1. 牛：_____个。　4. 龙：_____个。

2. 山羊：_____个。　5. 老虎：_____个。

3. 马：_____个。　6. 兔子：_____个。

山	羊	马	大	龙	田	老	水
小	生	龙	小	马	牛	虎	龙
牛	龙	小	田	生	龙	生	牛
水	生	水	龙	兔	子	田	马
龙	牛	龙	山	马	生	生	山
田	兔	老	大	龙	羊	龙	水
马	子	牛	虎	山	田	大	小
大	老	虎	龙	羊	龙	水	牛

Art Project: Chinese Zodiac Lantern
创意手工：生肖灯笼

Instructions:

1. Color the zodiac animals and lantern background.
2. Cut out the lantern shape.
3. Write the pinyin, character or next year number for each of the zodiac animals.

Note: Visit http://emarketing.cengageasia.com/cnywb for sample.

21

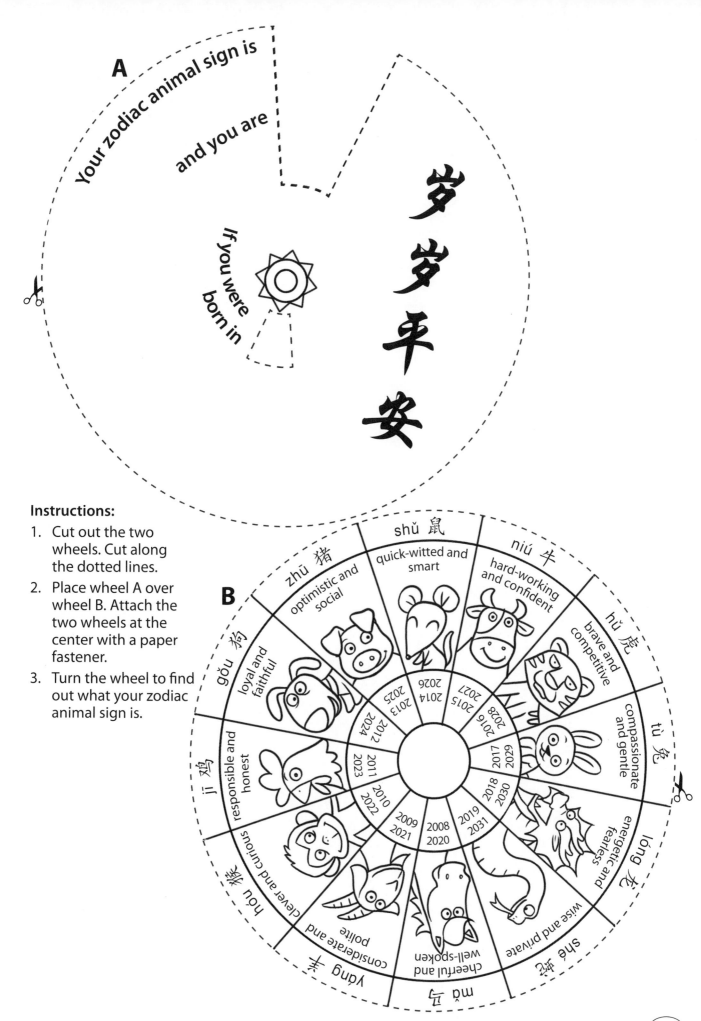

A

Your zodiac animal sign is

and you are

If you were born in

岁岁平安

Instructions:

1. Cut out the two wheels. Cut along the dotted lines.

2. Place wheel A over wheel B. Attach the two wheels at the center with a paper fastener.

3. Turn the wheel to find out what your zodiac animal sign is.

B

shǔ 鼠
quick-witted and smart

niú 牛
hard-working and confident

zhū 猪
optimistic and social

hǔ 虎
brave and competitive

gǒu 狗
loyal and faithful

tù 兔
compassionate and gentle

jī 鸡
responsible and honest

lóng 龙
energetic and fearless

hóu 猴
clever and curious

shé 蛇
wise and private

yáng 羊
considerate and polite

mǎ 马
cheerful and well-spoken

2012 2024
2013 2025
2014 2026
2015 2027
2016 2028
2017 2029
2018 2030
2019 2031
2011 2023
2010 2022
2009 2021
2008 2020

很久以前，中国有一个很聪明的皇帝。他管理全天下所有的事情。可是，皇帝渐渐老了，常常忘记事情，也忘记时间。他想了很久，终于想出了一个好办法。皇帝很喜欢动物，他想用十二种动物来计算时间。但是要如何挑选这十二种动物呢？为了公平起见，他决定举办一场赛跑。

第二天，皇帝召集所有的动物。他说："大家好！今天我们要举办一场动物赛跑，最先游过天河、跑到终点的十二只动物，可以代表我们中国来计算时间。依到达的顺序，每一只动物代表一年。每十二年重复一遍。"

赛跑开始了。所有的动物都拼命地跑。到了天河边，老鼠请求牛载它过河，牛答应了。当牛刚从水中上岸时，老鼠用力一跳，飞快地跑到了终点，因此老鼠得了第一名。随后是牛、虎、兔、龙、蛇、马、羊、猴、鸡、狗、猪。最后赛跑结束了。

这就是十二生肖的故事。

Long, long ago in the ancient Middle Kingdom which we know as China today, there lived a very wise emperor. The emperor was a very important man who had a lot of things on his mind because he had to take care of all the affairs of the people and creatures that lived in the Middle Kingdom. The emperor was getting older and so was becoming more and more forgetful. He was especially worried about how he was getting the years all mixed up in his mind. He couldn't remember the things that happened in each year.

One day while he was thinking about this problem, the emperor decided to name the years after animals because he loved animals. He felt that 12 would be a good number to pick, and, similar to a clock going round in rotation, the animals would also make a cycle. But he did not know which 12 animals to choose. The emperor was known to be a very fair ruler and did not believe he should choose his favorite animals. After some careful thought, he came up with a brilliant idea.

The next morning he called all the animals in the kingdom together and said, "Today we are going to have a great race. The first 12 animals to swim across the River of Heaven and cross the finish line will have the special honor of having a year named after them!"

Well, of course, all the animals were very excited because they all wanted to have a year named after them. The race began and the animals went as fast as they could. When it was time to cross the river, the clever rat, knowing that the ox was a strong swimmer, climbed on his back to get a free ride across the river. Just as the ox was climbing out of the river, the rat jumped off, hurried across the finish line and took first place.

After the rat, came the ox, tiger, rabbit, dragon, snake, horse, goat, monkey, rooster, dog, and finally the pig. The race ended. From this day on these 12 animals have had the special honor of having a year named for them.

Vocabulary Review: Story of the 12 Zodiac Animals
词汇练习：十二生肖的故事

Match the words in Column A with the words in Column B.

(Column A)

| 十二生肖 |
| shí èr shēng xiào |

| 请求 |
| qǐng qiú |

| 召集 |
| zhào jí |

| 聪明的 |
| cōng míng de |

| 最先 |
| zuì xiān |

| 结束 |
| jié shù |

| 开始 |
| kāi shǐ |

| 最后 |
| zuì hòu |

| 忘记 |
| wàng jì |

| 动物 |
| dòng wù |

| 赛跑 |
| sài pǎo |

| 重复 |
| chóng fù |

(Column B)

wise

ended

asked

animals

first

at last

race

repeated

summoned (called)

12 zodiac animals

began

forgot

Quiz: Story of the 12 Zodiac Animals
考考你：十二生肖的故事

动物	最先	最后	开始
结束	十二生肖	重复	请求
赛跑	忘记	聪明的	召集

1. 很久以前，中国有一个很＿＿＿＿＿＿皇帝。

2. 可是，皇帝渐渐老了，常常＿＿＿＿＿＿事情，也忘记时间。

3. 皇帝很喜欢＿＿＿＿＿＿，他想用十二种动物来计算时间。

4. 为了公平起见，他决定举办一场＿＿＿＿＿＿。
   ＿＿＿＿＿＿到达终点的动物可以代表中国计算时间。

5. 第二天，皇帝＿＿＿＿＿＿所有的动物。

6. 每一只动物代表一年。每十二年＿＿＿＿＿＿一遍。

7. 赛跑＿＿＿＿＿＿了。所有的动物都拼命地跑。

8. 到了天河边，老鼠＿＿＿＿＿＿牛载它过河。

9. ＿＿＿＿＿＿赛跑＿＿＿＿＿＿了，这就是＿＿＿＿＿＿的故事。

10. 依顺序写出十二生肖的名称：

＿＿＿＿＿＿、＿＿＿＿＿＿、＿＿＿＿＿＿、＿＿＿＿＿＿

＿＿＿＿＿＿、＿＿＿＿＿＿、＿＿＿＿＿＿、＿＿＿＿＿＿

＿＿＿＿＿＿、＿＿＿＿＿＿、＿＿＿＿＿＿、＿＿＿＿＿＿

Math Fun: Chinese Zodiac Animals
算一算，数一数：十二生肖

中国新年用十二种动物来代表，称为十二生肖。每一生肖代表一年，以鼠年开始，以猪年结束。然后再重复一次，顺序不变。

On the Chinese calendar, every year is represented by an animal. There are 12 zodiac animals that make a rotation. The cycle begins with the Rat and ends with the Pig. Each animal sign is repeated every 12 years and always follows the same order.

请回答下面问题：

Write the year on the Zodiac wheel and find out the answers below. Use the space above each zodiac animal to write the pinyin, character or year number for each of the zodiac animals.

jīn nián shì   nián   zhǎo chu nà ge shēng xiào   bìng tú shang hóng sè
1. 今年是_____年。找出那个生肖，并涂上红色。

qù nián shì   nián   zhǎo chu nà ge shēng xiào   bìng tú shang huáng sè
2. 去年是_____年。找出那个生肖，并涂上黄色。

míng nián shì   nián   zhǎo chu nà ge shēng xiào   bìng tú shang lán sè
3. 明年是_____年。找出那个生肖，并涂上蓝色。

sān nián qián shì   nián   zhǎo chu nà ge shēng xiào   bìng tú shang lǜ sè
4. 三年前是_____年。找出那个生肖，并涂上绿色。

shí èr nián hòu shì   nián
5. 十二年后是_____年。

挑战题（Challenge）：

1. 莉莉今年十岁，属马。他的哥哥属牛。
   莉莉的哥哥比她大_____岁。

shēng xiào
生肖

gōng xǐ fā cái
恭喜发财

biān pào
鞭炮

jiǎo zi
饺子

wǔ lóng wǔ shī
舞龙/舞狮

jú zi
桔子

shǒu suì
守岁
stay up late on New Year's Eve

yú
鱼

hóng bāo
红包

名字：＿＿＿＿＿＿＿＿＿＿＿＿＿＿　＿＿＿＿月＿＿＿＿日

Word Search: Chinese New Year
找一找：农历新年

Find the 11 pinyin words from the box below in the Word Search.

i	a	u	u	a	z	u	h	n	o	s
o	e	x	w	i	h	n	c	a	y	a
h	s	o	b	u	a	g	i	p	e	a
i	a	c	a	f	i	x	g	n	o	g
u	g	f	e	b	g	y	j	a	z	a
s	j	y	j	n	g	w	p	w	j	o
u	a	u	e	i	j	n	u	h	c	a
o	e	h	z	s	a	l	o	s	p	a
h	s	h	i	i	o	o	n	h	h	a
s	o	n	b	n	x	s	z	s	y	i
b	i	j	g	w	i	i	i	i	e	g

What do these words mean in English?

1. 春节 chūn jié: ＿＿＿＿＿＿＿＿＿＿

2. 红包 hóng bāo: ＿＿＿＿＿＿＿＿

3. 桔子 jú zi: ＿＿＿＿＿＿＿＿＿＿

4. 生肖 shēng xiào: ＿＿＿＿＿＿

5. 鞭炮 biān pào: ＿＿＿＿＿＿＿

6. 鱼 yú: ＿＿＿＿＿＿＿＿＿＿＿

7. 饺子 jiǎo zi: ＿＿＿＿＿＿＿＿

8. 舞狮 wǔ shī: ＿＿＿＿＿＿＿＿

9. 守岁 shǒu suì: ＿＿＿＿＿＿

10. 舞龙 wǔ lóng: ＿＿＿＿＿＿

11. 恭喜发财 gōng xǐ fā cái: ＿＿＿＿＿＿＿＿＿＿＿＿＿＿＿＿

Note: "春节" and "农历新年" both mean "Chinese New Year".

29

Vocabulary Review: Chinese New Year
词汇练习：农历新年

Fill in the blanks in pinyin or characters using the words below:

gōng xǐ fā cái 恭喜发财	shǒu suì 守岁	hóng bāo 红包	chūn jié 春节	jiǎo zi 饺子
wǔ lóng / wǔ shī 舞龙 / 舞狮	yú 鱼	shēng xiào 生肖	biān pào 鞭炮	jú zi 桔子

1. The animal signs related to people's age and personality.

2. The last dish served on Chinese New Year's Eve. It symbolizes surplus.

3. A food served on Chinese New Year's Eve. It symbolizes gold treasure.

4. A special lucky envelope that children receive from adults on Chinese New Year.

5. A special performance that brings good luck and is associated with drums and firecrackers.

6. A fruit served on Chinese New Year. Its name sounds like the word for good luck.

7. A kind of small explosive that creates noise and smoke that will scare the evil spirits away.

8. The custom of staying up late on Chinese New Year's Eve.

9. A popular greeting at Chinese New Year.

10. Another name for Chinese New Year.

dōng guā táng
冬瓜糖
winter melon candy

guā zi
瓜子
melon seeds

jīn jú
金桔
kumquats

guì yuán
桂圆
longan

huā shēng
花生
peanut

nián gāo
年糕
rice cake

fā gāo
发糕
steamed sponge cake

lián zi
莲子
lotus seeds

fèng lí sū
凤梨酥
pineapple tarts

Note: Festive snacks for Chinese New Year may vary in different parts of China.

Survey: What Food Do You Like to Eat During Chinese New Year?
问卷：你喜欢吃什么新年食品？

Using the dialogue below, conduct a survey in your class to find out which foods your classmates like to eat and which foods they do not like.

nǐ xǐ huan chī guā zi ma
Ⓐ 你喜欢吃瓜子吗？

wǒ xǐ huan bù xǐ huan chī guā zi
Ⓑ 我喜欢 / 不喜欢吃瓜子。

nǐ xǐ huan chī _____ ma
Ⓐ 你喜欢吃 _____ 吗？

wǒ xǐ huan bù xǐ huan chī
Ⓑ 我喜欢 / 不喜欢吃 _____ 。

dōng guā táng
冬瓜糖： Watermelon candy – symbolizing "sweetness".

guā zi
瓜子： Sunflower seeds – symbolizing "having many children".

jīn jú
金桔： Kumquat – symbolizing "luck" because kumquat and luck share the same sounds in Chinese.

guì yuán
桂圆： Dried longan – symbolizing "roundness" due to its round shape.

huā shēng
花生： Peanut – symbolizing "vitality and longevity".

nián gāo
年糕： Steamed rice cake – symbolizing "prosperity and promotion", because the word 高 (meaning "high") and 糕 share the same sound in Chinese.

fā gāo
发糕： Steamed sponge cake – symbolizing "higher promotion".

lián zi
莲子： Lotus seeds – symbolizing "having many children".

fèng lí sū
凤梨酥： Pineapple cake – symbolizing "wealth and prosperity" because it sounds like "To come forth, Prosperity!" in southern region dialect.

Rhyme: Chinese New Year Is Coming!
数来宝：新年到！

咚咚锵，咚咚锵，
咚咚咚锵咚咚咚锵。

Dōng dōng qiāng, dōng dōng qiāng,
dōng dōng dōng qiāng dōng dōng dōng qiāng.

(Sound imitation of the gongs and drums)

新年好，新年好。
穿新衣，戴新帽。
恭喜新年，春来到！

Xīn nián hǎo, xīn nián hǎo.
Chuān xīn yī, dài xīn mào.
Gōng xǐ xīn nián, chūn lái dào!

Happy New Year! Happy New Year!
Wear new clothes. Wear new hats.
Welcome the New Year. Welcome Spring!

* *

咚咚锵，咚咚锵，
咚咚咚锵咚咚咚锵。

Dōng dōng qiāng, dōng dōng qiāng,
dōng dōng dōng qiāng dōng dōng dōng qiāng.

(Sound imitation of the gongs and drums)

新年好，新年好。
拿红包，放鞭炮。
舞龙舞狮，真热闹！
真－热－闹！

Xīn nián hǎo, xīn nián hǎo.
Ná hóng bāo, fàng biān pào.
Wǔ lóng wǔ shī, zhēn rè nào!
Zhēn－rè－nào!

Happy New Year! Happy New Year!
Get the red envelopes. Set off the firecrackers.
Dragon dances, lion dances, so amazing!
A－M－A－Z－I－N－G!

读一读：

Can you read the following words?

新年

衣　　　帽

红包　　　鞭炮

舞龙舞狮　　真热闹

33

Reading: Story of Chinese New Year
读一读：年的故事

很久以前，在中国的一个山上，有一个怪物，它的名字叫"年"。"年"长得**又大又丑**。它有大大的嘴巴和尖尖的牙齿。每年的**除夕夜**，它会从山上下来**到处**找东西吃。村里的人们**发现**很多小孩不见了，**据说**是被"年"抓走了。因此，每年的除夕夜，大家都躲在屋里不敢出来。

有一年，村里来了一个老人。他告诉大家"年"最害怕三样东西：一是吵闹的声音，二是红颜色，三是火。如果**家家户户**都准备这三样东西，"年"就不敢来了。大家听了以后**打算**试试看。

到了除夕夜，大家都穿上红衣服，在门上贴红纸，在家门前打鼓，在街上放鞭炮。当"年"从山上下来时，它听到了吵闹的声音，看到了红颜色，并且到处都是火。它非常害怕，就飞快地跑回山上，再也不敢回到村里。

从此，每年的除夕夜，人们继续在门上贴红纸，并用鼓和鞭炮发出吵闹的声音。到现在这些做法就成为中国人迎接新年的传统**习俗**。

生词 Vocabulary

❶ 又大又丑 yòu dà yòu chǒu big and ugly	**❷ 除夕夜** chú xī yè New Year's Eve	**❸ 到处** dào chù everywhere	**❹ 发现** fā xiàn discover
❺ 家家户户 jiā jiā hù hù every household	**❻ 据说** jù shuō It is said	**❼ 打算** dǎ suàn plan to; intend	**❽ 习俗** xí sú customs

Fill in the blanks using words from the word bank.

据说	家家户户	除夕夜	到处
发现	又大又丑	习俗	打算

1. 村里的人们听了老人的话以后＿＿＿＿＿＿试试看。

2. "年"长得＿＿＿＿＿＿。

3. 村里的人们＿＿＿＿＿＿很多小孩不见了。

4. 如果＿＿＿＿＿＿都准备这三样东西，"年"就不敢来了。

5. ＿＿＿＿＿＿小孩子是被"年"抓走了。

6. 到现在这些做法就成为中国各地迎接新年的传统＿＿＿＿＿＿。

7. 每年的＿＿＿＿＿＿，"年"会从山上下来找东西吃。

8. 当"年"从山上下来时，它听到了吵闹的声音，看到了红颜色，并且＿＿＿＿＿＿都是火，它非常害怕。

In the mountains of China, long ago, there lived a terrible monster named Nian. Nian was big and ugly. It had a very large mouth and pointed teeth. Every year on New Year's Eve, Nian would go from the top of the mountain into the village and find something to eat. Each year people in the village found that many children were missing, and it was said that they were taken away by Nian. Therefore, every year on New Year's Eve, the frightened villagers hid in their homes and dared not come out.

One year, an old man came to the village. He told everyone that Nian was frightened by three things: one is noise, the second is red color, and the third is fire. He told the villagers that each household should use these three things on New Year's Eve to keep Nian away from the village. After listening to the old man, they all agreed to give it a try.

On New Year's Eve, everyone put on red clothes, put red paper on their doors, beat drums in front of their houses, and set off firecrackers in the streets. This time when Nian came, it heard noises, saw the color red and fire everywhere. It was very scared and ran back to the mountains quickly, never to return to the village again.

Ever since that time, the villagers continued their practice of covering their homes with red decorations and making loud noises with drums and firecrackers on the night before the New Year. This practice has become the traditional way to welcome in the New Year everywhere in China.

guò xīn nián
过新年
Chinese New Year Celebration

名字：＿＿＿＿＿＿＿＿＿

wǒ men dà sǎo chú　　qù jiù yíng xīn
我们大扫除，去旧迎新。
We c＿＿＿＿＿＿ the house and s＿＿＿＿＿＿ the floor.
It is time to get rid of the old and welcome the ＿＿＿＿＿＿ year.

wǒ men tiē chūn lián   jiǎn chūn huā   dà jí dà lì

我们贴春联，剪春花，大吉大利。

We put up red c_____ and p_____ c_____ on doors and windows for good luck.

wǒ men mǎi xīn yī fu   jiǎn tóu fa   xīn nián kuài lè

我们买新衣服，剪头发，新年快乐。

We buy new c_____ and get h_____ to start the new year.

On Chinese New Year's Eve

wǒ men huí jiā chī nián yè fàn　　tuán tuán yuán yuán

我们回家吃年夜饭，团团圆圆。

We go home for a big family r_____ dinner on New Year's Eve.

wǒ men chī jī　　yā　　yú　　jiǎo zi　　nián gāo hé huǒ guō

我们吃鸡、鸭、鱼、饺子、年糕和火锅，

jí xiáng rú yì

吉祥如意。

We eat c_____, d_____, f_____, d_____,

rice cakes and hotpots. All are symbolic of good luck and wealth.

On Chinese New Year

wǒ men xiàng dà ren bài nián　　suì suì píng ān

我们向大人拜年，岁岁平安。

We say "G_____" to grown-ups and receive red _____ for good luck.

wǒ men fàng biān pào　　kàn wǔ lóng wǔ shī　　qìng zhù xīn nián

我们放鞭炮，看舞龙舞狮，庆祝新年。

We set off the _____ and watch the lion dance and dragon parade to celebrate the New Year.

Character Code Challenge: Chinese New Year Message ❶
解码游戏：新年密语 ⚫

Use the character codes below to solve the secret message about Chinese New Year.

A：一	B：二	C：三	D：四	E：五	F：六
G：七	H：八	I：九	J：十	K：口	L：手
M：人	N：天	O：木	P：心	Q：日	R：月
S：山	T：水	U：火	V：上	W：下	X：大
Y：小	Z：中				

下五　下五一月　月五四　六木月

七木木四　手火三口　一天四　水木

山三一月五　一下一小　五上九手

山心九月九水山

yī 一 one	èr 二 two	sān 三 three	sì 四 four	wǔ 五 five	liù 六 six	qī 七 seven
bā 八 eight	jiǔ 九 nine	shí 十 ten	kǒu 口 mouth	shǒu 手 hand	rén 人 person	tiān 天 sky
mù 木 wood	xīn 心 heart	rì 日 sun	yuè 月 moon	shān 山 mountain	shuǐ 水 water	huǒ 火 fire
shàng 上 up	xià 下 down	dà 大 big	xiǎo 小 small	zhōng 中 middle		

Character Code Challenge: Chinese New Year Message ❷
解码游戏：新年密语 ⚫

Use the character codes below to solve the secret message about Chinese New Year.

A：木	**B**：月	**C**：下	**D**：田	**E**：手	**F**：一
G：火	**H**：人	**I**：小	**J**：男	**K**：口	**L**：二
M：水	**N**：大	**O**：牛	**P**：耳	**Q**：子	**R**：三
S：山	**T**：上	**U**：女	**V**：目	**W**：心	**X**：四
Y：日	**Z**：中				

心人牛二手　一小山人　木三手　山手三目手田

心小上人　上人手　人手木田山　木大田　上木小二山

牛大　上牛　山日水月牛二小中手　人木耳耳日

月手火小大大小大火山　木大田

手大田小大火山

mù	yuè	xià	tián	shǒu	yī	huǒ
木 wood	月 moon	下 down	田 field	手 hand	一 one	火 fire
rén	xiǎo	nán	kǒu	èr	shuǐ	dà
人 person	小 small	男 man	口 mouth	二 two	水 water	大 big
niú	ěr	zǐ	sān	shān	shàng	nǚ
牛 cow	耳 ear	子 child	三 three	山 mountain	上 up	女 female
mù	xīn	sì	rì	zhōng		
目 eye	心 heart	四 four	日 sun	中 middle		

Art Project: Lucky Messages for New Year
创意手工：新年吉祥话

Instructions:
1. Read and discuss the meaning of these sayings with your classmates.
2. Choose your favorite saying and practice writing it.

dà　jí　dà　lì
大吉大利
May you have lots of good luck and fortune.

jí　xiáng　rú　yì
吉祥如意
May you have good fortune in all your affairs.

chū　rù　píng　ān
出入平安
May you have peace wherever you go.

sì　jì　píng　ān
四季平安
May you have peace throughout the four seasons.

wǔ　fú　lín　mén
五福临门
May the five good fortunes come through your door.

lǎo　shǎo　píng　ān
老少平安
May everyone in your family be safe and sound.

Art Project: Chinese New Year Couplets
创意手工：对联

Note: *See instructions on the reverse page.*

Instructions:

1. Enlarge and copy the templates on page 41 on red paper.
2. Choose two of the sayings on page 40 and copy them with pencil onto the template paper.
3. Go over the characters with a gold paint pen, a black marker, or a writing brush.
4. Hang the couplets on the sides of the door frames at school or home to bring good luck.

Instructions:

1. Color and cut out the dragon picture.
2. Paste the dragon's head onto the base flap of a folded brown paper bag.
3. Attach four 3″x2″ pieces of colorful tissue or crepe paper to the sides of the bag.
4. Write the character "龙" on the front of the paper bag.

Note: Visit http://emarketing.cengageasia.com/cnywb for sample.

名字：＿＿＿＿＿＿＿＿＿＿ ＿＿＿月＿＿＿日

Instructions:

1. Trace a template of 9" circle on red construction paper to make the body of the fish.
2. Cut out a triangle from the circle to form a mouth.
3. Staple the small triangle piece to the opposite side to form a tail.
4. Color the picture of the fish above. Cut it out and paste it in the center of the red fish.
5. Add a fish eye above the mouth.
6. Decorate the fish with a pattern or a lucky message.

Note: Visit http://emarketing.cengageasia.com/cnywb for sample.

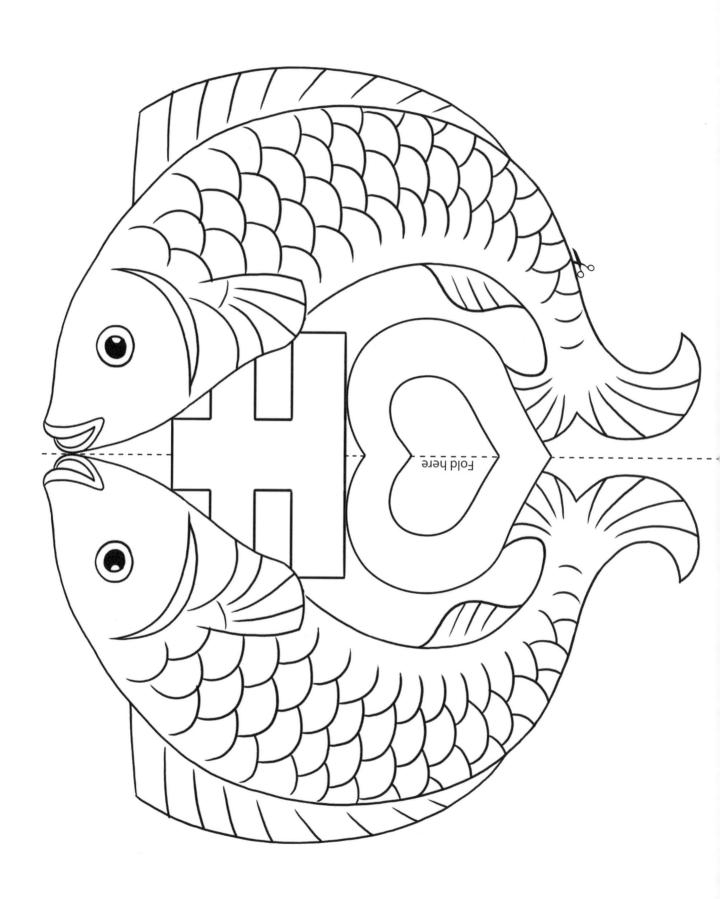

Instructions:

1. Color the fish.
2. Fold the paper in half on the dotted line with the illustration facing out.
3. Keeping the paper folded, cut around the outside of the fish and then cut out the inside pieces.
4. Paste the fish diagonally onto a 9″ square of red paper.
5. Hang the paper-cut for display.

名字： _____   _____月 _____日

Instructions:

1. Make copies of this template on yellow or red paper if possible.
2. Fold in half along the dotted line and cut along the black lines.
3. Open up and paste diagonally onto a 9″ square of red construction paper (use the reverse side to hide the dotted line).
4. Display the decorations horizontally or vertically.

Note: Visit http://emarketing.cengageasia.com/cnywb for sample.

Art Project: Red Envelope
创意手工：红包

A hongbao is a red envelope decorated with gold writing or pictures. It contains lucky money and is a traditional Chinese New Year's gift for children. Below is a template for making your own hongbao.

Flap

Paste to A

A

Paste to B

B

Instructions:

1. Cut out the envelope template.
2. Fold along the dotted lines and paste where indicated.
3. Decorate with popular New Year symbols such as fish, zodiac animals, firecrackers, and/or lucky messages.

Note: Visit http://emarketing.cengageasia.com/cnywb for sample.

Art Project: Go Green Flower
创意手工：环保花

Instructions:

Materials needed: 6 red envelopes (红包), 1 bottle cap, glue or transparent tape.

1. Fold each envelope to make petals as shown. Tape each one to hold shape in place.
2. Arrange the petals into a circle shape and tape them together.
3. Glue or tape small triangles of scrap paper to the inside of a bottle cap and tape it in the middle of the flower.
4. Cut out leaves from green paper and glue or tape them to the back of the flower.

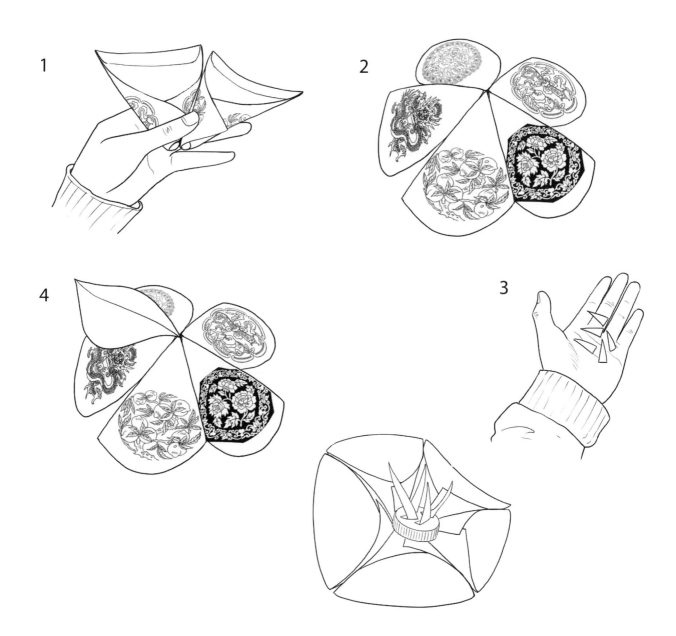

Art Project: Palace Lantern
创意手工：宫灯

Instructions:

1. Color the lantern template in red or copy the template on red copy paper.
2. At the top of the lantern, write the year, the zodiac animal name in Chinese (and English).
3. In the three diamond shapes, write a character for good fortune, peace, or spring, etc.
4. Write couplets on the two sides of the doors. If gold paint pens are available, write all in pencil first, then go over everything with a gold pen. If not, another colored marker can be used.

Art Project: Firecrackers
创意手工：鞭炮

1

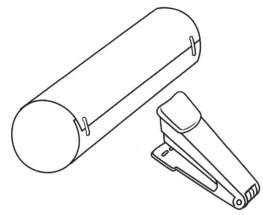

2

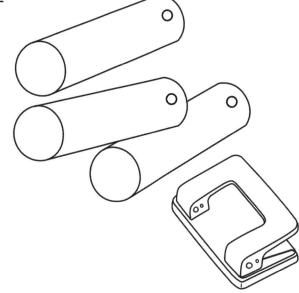

Materials needed:

- Red paper 3" x 4" – 6 pieces
- Red paper 2" x 6" – 1 piece
- Red yarn 1 ½ ft. – 1 piece

Instructions:

1. Roll and staple each of the 3"x4" pieces of red paper to form tubes.
2. Punch a hole on the top of each tube.
3. Thread the yarn into each hole and make a knot.
4. Write a lucky message on the big red paper and tie it to the tail.

3

4

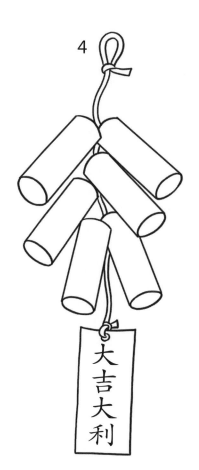

Note: Visit http://emarketing.cengageasia.com/cnywb for sample.

名字：＿＿＿＿＿

月＿＿＿日

Note: See instructions on the reverse page.

Who can reach the Dragon's Head first?

一 二 三 四 五 六 七 八 九 十 十一 十二 十三 十四 十五 十六 十七 十八 十九 二十 二十一 二十二 二十三 二十四 二十五 二十六 二十七 二十八 二十九 三十 三十一

Different ways to play:

1. To make game cards about Chinese New Year trivia, use page 53.

2. To play the game with questions about zodiac animals, students who can translate the animals from Chinese to English or vice versa can move toward the Dragon's head.

3. To play the game with questions about Chinese numbers, prepare index cards with numbers 1-30 written in Chinese or English.

4. To play the game with solving math problems, the teacher can write a math problem on each dragon section.

5. This dragon design can also be used as a coloring activity. The teacher can use a color code such as color sections 1, 3, 5, 12 in red; color sections 2, 9, 20, 23 in green and so on, preferably in Chinese. Students can also be given the option of making their own color code.

Game: Chinese New Year Qs and As
问答游戏：农历新年知多少

今年是什么生肖年？ What is the animal sign for this year? **2 Points**	一共有几个生肖？ How many Zodiac animals are there? **2 Points**	动物赛跑，谁跑第一名？ Who is the winner in the Zodiac Race? **1 Point**
十二生肖最后一名是谁？ Who is the 12th winner in the Zodiac Race? **2 Points**	十二生肖里有没有猫？ Is the cat one of the Zodiac animals? **2 Points**	今年农历新年是几月几日？ When is Chinese New Year this year? **3 Points**
新年的吉祥颜色是什么？ What is the good luck color for Chinese New Year? **1 Point**	小孩子过年会收到什么礼物？ What do children receive from adults on Chinese New year? **2 Points**	农历新年又叫什么？ What is the other name for Chinese New Year? **3 Points**
鱼在过年时代表什么？ What does fish symbolize in Chinese New Year? **2 Points**	为什么过年要穿红衣服和新衣服？ Why do Chinese people wear red and new clothes on Chinese New Year? **1 Point**	红包里面装了什么？ What is inside the red envelopes? **1 Point**
为什么过年要放鞭炮？ Why do Chinese people light firecrackers during Chinese New Year? **2 Points**	元宵节是什么时候？ When is the Lantern Festival? **2 Points**	请说一句新年吉祥话。 Say one good luck greeting in Chinese. **3 Points**

Song: Happy New Year!
新年歌：恭喜！恭喜！

měi tiáo dà jiē xiǎo xiàng
每条大街 小 巷，
Up and down the streets today,

měi gè rén de zuǐ li
每个人的 嘴 里，
Happy people on their way,

jiàn miàn dì yí jù huà
见面第一 句 话，
Upon meeting, they will say,

jiù shì gōng xǐ gōng xǐ
就是恭喜 恭 喜。
"Gong Xi, Gong Xi, Gong Xi."

gōng xǐ gōng xǐ   gōng xǐ nǐ ya
恭喜恭喜 恭喜你呀！
Gong Xi, Gong Xi, Gong Xi ni ya!

gōng xǐ gōng xǐ   gōng xǐ nǐ
恭喜恭喜 恭喜你！
Gong Xi, Gong Xi, Gong Xi ni!

54

Recipe: Dumplings
下厨乐：包饺子

Ingredients

1 lb. Chinese cabbage

2 scallions

2 cloves of garlic, finely chopped

2 tsp. fresh ginger, finely chopped

1 tbsp. soy sauce

1 tbsp sesame oil

1 tsp. salt

1 tbsp. cornstarch

1 lb. lean ground pork

1 10-oz. package prepared dumpling wrappers (available at Asian food stores)

Steps

Part 1:

1. Finely chop the Chinese cabbage and scallions and put them in a mixing bowl.
2. Add the soy sauce, salt, cornstarch, and pork. Mix well with a spoon.
3. Place 1 teaspoon of filling on each wrapper.
4. Fold the wrappers into half circles. Moisten the edges with water, and press them together to seal.

Part 2:

1. In a large pot, bring 2 quarts of water to a boil.
2. Put in the dumplings and cover the pot. When the water starts boiling, add 1 cup of cold water.
3. Repeat this step twice. When the water boils for the third time, the dumplings are done.
4. Serve with 1/4 cup of soy sauce mixed with 2 tablespoons of vinegar. Makes 4 dozen dumplings.

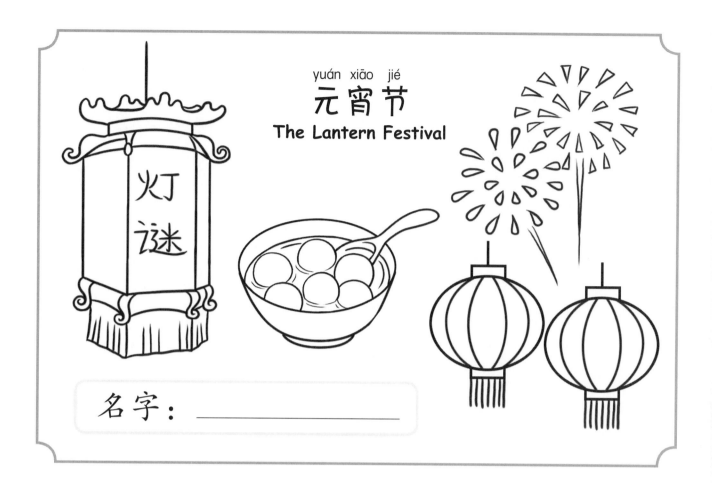

yuán xiāo jié
元宵节
The Lantern Festival

名字：＿＿＿＿＿＿＿＿＿＿＿

一

zhēng yuè shí wǔ shì yuán xiāo jié　　tā shì chūn jié de zuì hòu yì tiān
正月十五是元宵节。它是春节的最后一天。

The ＿＿＿＿＿＿＿＿ day of Chinese New Year is the ＿＿＿＿＿＿＿＿ Festival.
It marks an end to the 15 day period of Chinese New Year celebration.

zhè   yì   tiān shì xīn nián yǐ   hòu kàn dào de   dì   yí   gè mǎn yuè

这一天是新年以后看到的第一个满月。

On this day, we see the first f_____ m_____ of the New Year.

wǒ men chī   yuán xiāo   dài biǎo quán jiā tuán yuán

我们吃"元宵"代表全家团圆。

We eat sweet, round dumplings called "_____ _____" to symbolize family togetherness.

wǒ men shàng jiē qù kàn huā dēng wǔ lóng hé yān huǒ
我们上街去看花灯、舞龙和烟火。
People dress up and head to the street to see l_____,
dragon _____, and f_____.

外黄内白，
猴子最爱。
（猜一水果）
Yellow outside,
white inside.
Monkey's favorite
treat. (a fruit)

wǒ men cāi dēng mí zhēn yǒu qù
我们猜灯谜，真有趣。
We guess _____ attached to lanterns. It is a lot of fun for everyone.

名字：＿＿＿＿＿＿＿＿＿＿＿＿＿＿＿　＿＿＿＿月＿＿＿＿日

Art Project: Chinese New Year Lantern
创意手工：新年灯笼

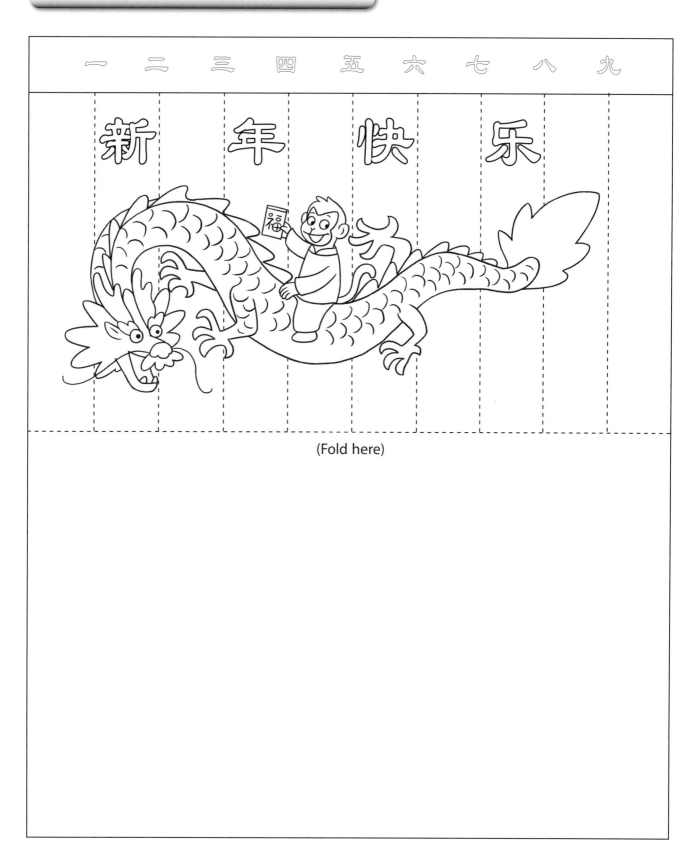

(Fold here)

Note: See instructions on the reverse page. Visit http://emarketing.cengageasia.com/cnywb for sample.

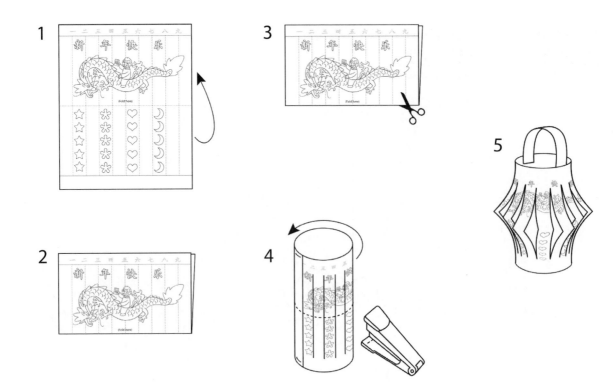

Instructions:

1. Color the image and the Chinese characters for "新年快乐"; decorate the lower half of the template with other patterns and color them.
2. Fold along the line where indicated.
3. Cut along the dotted lines, while keeping paper folded.
4. Roll to make a lantern shape and staple the ends together.
5. Staple a 6"x2" strip of red paper across the top to make a handle.

Art Project: Chinese Lantern Paper Cut
创意手工：灯笼剪纸

Follow the instructions below to make this paper cut.

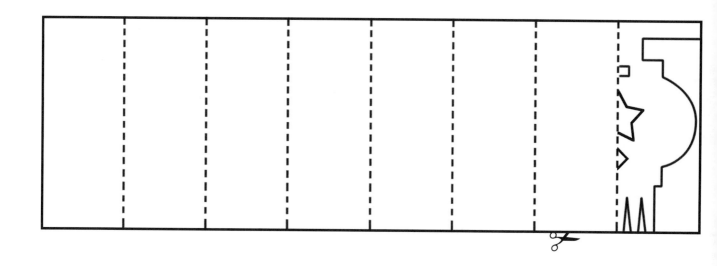

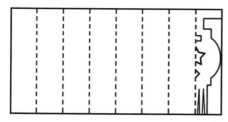

1. Cut out the whole piece of paper.

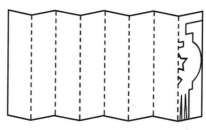

2. Fold along the dotted lines.

3. Maintaining the folds, cut out the shape of the lantern.

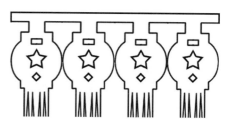

4. Unfold the paper to get the Chinese lantern paper cut.

Note: Visit http://emarketing.cengageasia.com/cnywb for sample.

Riddle Game: Riddles for Lantern Festival
猜一猜：趣味灯谜

1.
没根不用种，打开像朵花，
四季都会开。（猜一物）

It can grow but has no roots,
Opens like a flower,
Seen all year round.
(an object)

2.
有风不用它，没风可生风，不动
不凉，越动越凉。（猜一物）

It is useless when it is windy,
It makes wind when there is none,
When you don't move it, it is not cool,
When you move it, it becomes cool.
(an object)

3.
两只脚一样长，
甜酸苦辣一起尝。（猜一物）

It has two feet of the same length.
It takes up everything sweet, sour,
bitter or spicy.
(an object)

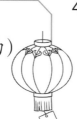
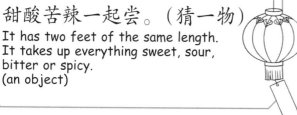

4.
头上几根羽毛，人人拿来玩，
最爱空中跳舞。（猜一物）

It has a few feathers on its head,
Everyone likes to play with it,
It loves to dance in the air.
(an object)

5.
嘴长肚子大，不吃饭和菜，
爱喝白开水，也爱吐黄水。
（猜一日常用品）

Long mouth and big belly; does not eat rice
or vegetables; loves to drink clear water;
yellow water pours from it. (an object)

6.
门边贴上红彩衣，一左一右
写满字，喜庆日子便出来。
（猜一物）

Two red strips stuck on two sides of the
door; left and right, each filled with words;
they show up on happy occasions. (an object)

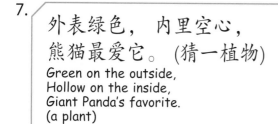

7.
外表绿色，内里空心，
熊猫最爱它。（猜一植物)

Green on the outside,
Hollow on the inside,
Giant Panda's favorite.
(a plant)

8.
圆形两兄弟，长得一样高，
互追追不到，合作向前走。
（猜一物）

Like two round-shaped brothers; exactly the
same height; always chasing each other; and
working together to move forward. (an object)

9.
身体用纸造，纸里包住火，
拿着夜行乐趣多。（猜一物）

Its body is made of paper,
Fire fills its inside,
Lots of fun to hold at night.
(an object)

10.
白里透红，生日祝寿。
（猜一食品）

White inside and red outside,
Eaten on birthdays for long life.
(a food)

名字：_____ _____月_____日

11.
脖子能伸缩，手脚可收藏，
水陆能生存，一生寿命长。
（猜一动物）
Its neck can stretch.
Its feet can hide.
It can survive in water and on land.
It has a long life. (an animal)

12.
白宝宝，爱吃叶，自筑房子，
人们作衣裳。（猜一昆虫）
It has a white body.
It loves to eat leaves.
It builds its own home.
People use it to make clothes.
(an insect)

13.
身结红果，引它发火，
声大如雷，好运便来。
（猜一物）
Its body is covered in red; when lit, it
lights up the sky; sounds like loud thunder;
makes good luck come your way. (an object)

14.
日吃数十斤，初生粉红皮，
渐成黑白衣，圆圆胖胖好
脾气。（猜一动物）
Eats a lot every day; pink when it is
born; gradually turns black and white;
chubby and cheerful. (an animal)

15.
皮制面皮，肚子空心，
不打不发声，越打越欢喜。
（猜一物）
Leather skin. Hollow belly. If you don't
beat it, it has no sound. If you beat it
hard enough, it feels happy. (an object)

16.
有时像桔子，有时像香蕉，
看得见，摸不到。
（猜一自然景象）
Sometimes it looks like an orange. Sometimes
it looks like a banana. You can see it, but you
cannot touch it. (a natural thing)

17.
兄弟两个，一东一西，
可以听到，不能见到。
（猜一脸上器官）
Two brothers, one right, one left.
They hear each other, but they cannot
see each other. (a sense organ)

18.
外黄内白，猴子最爱。
（猜一水果）
Yellow outside, white inside.
Monkey's favorite treat.
(a fruit)

19.
可大可小，可长可短。
只能前进，不能退后。
(猜一抽象物)
They can be big or small, long or short.
They can only go forward. They cannot go
backward. (an abstract concept)

20.
有面没有口，有脚没有手。
虽有四只脚，自己不会走。
（猜一物）
It has a face but no mouth. It has legs
but no hands. Even though it has four
legs, it cannot walk. (an object)

Try It Out: Let's Talk!
练一练：说一说

Dialogue 1

Ⓐ
nǐ shì nǎ yì nián chū shēng de
你是哪一年出生的？

Ⓑ
wǒ shì   chū shēng de
我是＿＿＿＿＿＿出生的。

Ⓐ
nà nǐ shǔ shén me
那你属什么？

Ⓑ
wǒ shǔ
我属＿＿＿＿＿＿。

Dialogue 2

Ⓐ
nǐ zuì xǐ huan nǎ yí gè shēng xiào
你最喜欢哪一个生肖？

Ⓑ
wǒ zuì xǐ huan
我最喜欢＿＿＿＿＿＿。

Ⓐ
wèi shén me
为什么？

Ⓑ
yīn wèi
因为＿＿＿＿＿＿

yòu   yòu
又＿＿＿＿＿又＿＿＿＿＿。

Dialogue 3

Ⓐ
guò xīn nián yào shuō shén me jí xiáng huà
过新年要说什么吉祥话？

Ⓑ
xīn nián kuài lè   gōng xǐ fā cái
新年快乐！恭喜发财！

Ⓐ
nǐ huì zěn me qìng zhù xīn nián
你会怎么庆祝新年？

Ⓑ ＿＿＿＿＿＿＿＿＿＿＿＿＿＿＿

(Mention at least two activities.)

Try It Out: Let's Write!
练一练：写一写

天 tiān sky

Useful Words

tiān kōng	tiān qì
天空	天气
sky	weather

天 天 天 天

天

天

Try It Out: Let's Write!
练一练：写一写

米 岺 米 米 **米** mǐ
rice

Useful Words

mǐ fàn	mǐ fěn
米饭	米粉
rice	rice noodles

米 米 米 米 米 米

米

米

Try It Out: Let's Write!
练一练：写一写

早　　　早　　　昂　　　早 zǎo
early

Useful Words

zǎo shang	zǎn cān
早上	早餐
morning	breakfast

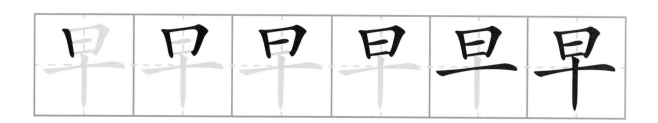

早　早　早　早　早　早

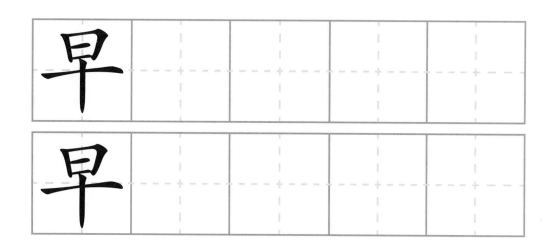

早

早

Try It Out: Let's Write!
练一练：写一写

年

nián
year

Useful Words

nián qīng	xīn nián
年轻	新年
young	New Year

年

Try It Out: Let's Write!
练一练：写一写

吉 *jí*
good luck

Useful Words

dà jí
大吉
good luck

jí xiáng
吉祥
auspicious

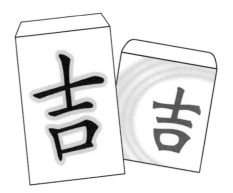

吉 吉 吉 吉 吉 吉

吉

吉

Try It Out: Let's Write!
练一练：写一写

斄　𦬩　𦰩　春 chūn
spring

Useful Words

chūn tiān
春天
spring

chūn jié
春节
Chinese New Year

春　春　春　春　春　春

春　春　春

春

春

Try It Out: Let's Write!
练一练：写一写

畐 福 福 福

fú
fortune

Useful Words

fú qì	fú xīng
福气	福星
blessing	lucky star

福 福 福 福 福 福 福

福 福 福 福 福 福

福

福

Vocabulary Review: Who Am I?
词汇练习：我是谁? *(page 11)*

1. 鸡	2. 老鼠	3. 龙	4. 老虎
5. 马	6. 猪	7. 蛇	8. 兔子
9. 羊	10. 狗	11. 牛	12. 猴子

Mini-Book: What Can These Animals Do?
我的小书：它们能（会）做什么?
(pages 13–15)

图五：吃	图六：拉	图七：爬
图八：跳	图九：飞	图十：游泳
图十一：跑	图十二：吃	图十三：爬
图十五：吠	图十六：睡觉	

Math Skills: Fill in the Missing Zodiac Animal Years 算一算：填写生肖年份? *(page 17)*

虎；2007年，猪

Word Search: Zodiac Animals ❶
找一找：生肖 一 *(page 19)*

1. 猪: pig	2. 老虎: tiger	3. 鸡: rooster
4. 老鼠: rat	5. 马: horse	6. 兔子: rabbit
7. 牛: ox	8. 蛇: snake	9. 龙: dragon
10. 猴子: monkey	11. 羊: goat	12. 狗: dog

```
c j l m z k l i g t c i a
g n i e o a a x b k w z
c l u t d i d m o l y h c
n i l e i a m e d h u o e
n t e k a g e m l n u u g
h a x h c y c d y a n z b
g p k e p g t y l g d i h
x y a n g y u g o u j t m
p w d s y h j m n s a c a e
k b x i s i b e g u b u e h
c s d o a y e k m l y d h
l v a e x h y c m t i h b
i l y d h c o g o z h a g
h s g m u s t x u j o l c
k d y h u m k t o h d j e
```

Word Search: Zodiac Animals ❷
找一找：生肖 二 *(page 20)*

1. 牛 : 6个	4. 龙 : 12个
2. 山羊 : 3个	5. 老虎 : 3个
3. 马 : 5个	6. 兔子 : 2个

山	羊	马	大	龙	田	老	水
小	生	龙	小	马	牛	虎	龙
牛	龙	小	田	生	龙	生	牛
水	生	水	龙	兔	子	田	马
龙	牛	龙	山	马	生	生	山
田	兔	老	大	龙	羊	龙	水
马	子	牛	虎	山	田	大	小
大	老	虎	龙	羊	龙	水	牛

Vocabulary Review: Story of the 12 Zodiac Animals 词汇练习：十二生肖的故事
(page 25)

十二生肖 – 12 zodiac animals

请求 – asked

召集 – summoned (called)

聪明的 – wise	忘记 – forgot
最先 – first	动物 – animals
结束 – ended	赛跑 – race
开始 – began	重复 – repeated

最后 – at last

Quiz: Story of the 12 Zodiac Animals
考考你：十二生肖的故事 *(page 26)*

1. 聪明	2. 忘记	3. 动物
4. 赛跑、最先	5. 召集	6. 重复
7. 开始	8. 请求	

9. 最后、结束、十二生肖

10. 鼠、牛、虎、兔、龙、蛇、
马、羊、猴、鸡、狗、猪

Answer Key 答案

Math Fun: Chinese Zodiac Animals
算一算，数一数：十二生肖 *(page 27)*

挑战题答案：五

Word Search: Chinese New Year
找一找：农历新年 *(page 29)*

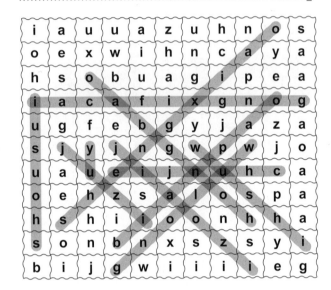

Vocabulary Review: Chinese New Year
词汇练习：农历新年 *(page 30)*

1. 生肖　　2. 鱼　　3. 饺子　　4. 红包

5. 舞龙 / 舞狮　　6. 桔子　　7. 鞭炮

8. 守岁　　9. 恭喜发财　　10. 春节

Reading: Story of Chinese New Year
读一读：年的故事 *(page 35)*

1. 打算　　2. 又大又丑　　3. 发现

4. 家家户户　　5. 据说　　6. 习俗

7. 除夕夜　　8. 到处

Mini-Book: Chinese New Year Celebration
我的小书：过新年 *(pages 36–39)*

Picture 1: clean, sweep, new
Picture 2: couplets, paper, cuts
Picture 3: clothes, haircuts
Picture 4: reunion

Picture 5: chicken, duck, fish, dumplings
Picture 6: Gong Xi Fa Cai, envelopes
Picture 7: firecrackers

Character Code Challenge: Chinese New Year Message ❶ 解码游戏：新年密语 一 *(page 40)*

We wear red for good luck and to scare away evil spirits.

Character Code Challenge: Chinese New Year Message ❷ 解码游戏：新年密语 二 *(page 41)*

Whole fish are served with the heads and tails on to represent happy beginnings and endings.

Mini-Book: The Lantern Festival
我的小书：元宵节 *(pages 56-58)*

Picture 1: fifteenth, Lantern
Picture 2: full, moon
Picture 3: yuan, xiao
Picture 4: lanterns, dance, fireworks
Picture 5: riddles.

Riddle Game: Riddles for Lantern Festival
猜一猜：趣味灯谜 *(pages 61-62)*

1. 雨伞 (umbrella)　　2. 扇子 (fan)

3. 筷子 (chopsticks)　　4. 毽子 (shuttlecock)

5. 茶壶 (teapot)　　6. 对联 (couplets)

7. 竹子 (bamboo)　　8. 自行车 (bicycle)

9. 灯笼 (lantern)　　10. 寿桃 (peach)

11. 乌龟 (turtle)　　12. 蚕 (silkworm)

13. 鞭炮 (firecrackers)　　14. 熊猫 (panda)

15. 鼓 (drum)　　16. 月亮 (moon)

17. 耳朵 (ears)　　18. 香蕉 (banana)

19. 年龄 (age)　　20. 桌子 (table)